Dominick Argento
Cabaret Songs

for Medium Voice and Piano

DISTRIBUTED BY

HAL•LEONARD®
CORPORATION
7777 W. BLUEMOUND RD. P.O. BOX 13819 MILWAUKEE, WI 53213

www.boosey.com
www.halleonard.com

CONTENTS

* When programmed as a group, '5a. You' should be listed simply
as '5. You' and the following two titles unlisted.

1. WHO COULD HAVE KNOWN?

Who could have known
That we'd end up like this?
Who knew that you
Would change my blues to bliss?

Who could express
All that you mean to me?
Deeds pale, words fail,
To convey my love's immensity.

During all those years,
We'd nod and grin,
  then go our ways, apart.
We used the language
Old friends speak in
  'till we learned the language of the heart
  (When it sings).

Who would have known
I could start life anew?
It's clear, my dear,
Now that you are here, it was you.

2. YOU ARE A LOVE SONG

You are a love song
I hear all the time.
The words — short and simple:
"I'm yours. You're mine."
A song that will resonate
As long as life endures.
In tones as sweet as you are:
"You're mine. I'm yours."

Though the heart is mute
It found a way
Through the pow'r of music
To convey
"I'm yours. You're mine."
What more is there to say?

Our song will reverberate
Eternally, a sign
To tell the world
Who we are:
"I'm yours. You're mine!"

3. THE LUCKIEST WOMAN

I never won the lottery,
Or a prize of any worth.
And yet to me I'll always be
The luckiest woman on earth.

I'm hopeless at Monopoly
And at cards I vainly strive.
But nonetheless, I must confess,
I'm the luckiest woman alive.

I wash the car; it's sure to rain.
Invest my dough; right down the drain.
Get a great job Monday; Tuesday: fired.
Go to pay my bill; find the credit card's expired
  a month ago! Oh, no! Oh, no!

But damnit! I reiterate
I'm as lucky as can be,
'Cause neither fame nor fortune compensate
For all that your love means to me.

4. SAI TU PERCHÈ

Sai tu perchè la luna splende?
Do you know why the moon is glowing?
Sai tu perchè il sole brilla?
Do you know why the sun's so bright?
Perchè riflettano la luce d'un amor,
Because they are reflecting the light of a love,
La luce d'un amore grande quant'e la mia.
The light of a love as great as mine.

Non trovo mai parole giuste;
I can never find the proper words;
Non potrei dirti quanto t'amo.
I'm unable to tell you how much I love you.
Ma se tu vuoi saper i miei ver pensier,
But if you wish to know my truest thoughts,
Bisogna legger quel ch'è scritto nel cuore mio.
You must read what is written in my heart.

Ed ecco cos'è scritto
And this is what it says:

"Senza te fianc'a fianco con me
"Without you side by side with me
Il cuore romperebbe;
My heart would break;
Senza te nelle bracce di me
Without you in my arms
La vita finerebbe."
My life would end."

Solo tu mi fa contento,
You alone can make me happy,
Tu sei la musica che sento.
You are the music that I hear.
La luna ed il sol aiutano narrar
The moon and sun are helping to narrate
La storia d'un amore grande come la nostra.
The story of a love as great as ours.

5a. YOU

You are the gift Love sent to charm my days.
Your smile can disarm me in a thousand
  diff'rent ways.
At times we sit and reminisce.
You talk of that, I talk of this.
And I am at my happiest whenever there's
  a chance to simply gaze and gaze at You!

You're the reason that my heart's so light.
The love that you show me makes my future feel
  as bright
As blue skies on a sunny day and schoolboys on
  a holiday.
One person makes me feel that way and that is you.

Thanks to you I now believe that miracles come true:
I ask you what you're thinking. You reply: "It's
  always you."
At first we were uncertain yet when all is said and done,
Love is better late than never. Now's our moment in
  the sun.

O You, you are music, a tremendous theme,
Mere words are unworthy to describe so dear a dream,
I'll never have my fill of you, the endless joy and
  thrill of you,
I'll keep right on until you too say "I'm in love
  with you!"

5b. CRAZY LADY (Ripostc*)

Crazy lady, losin' her mind!
She thinks love guides her.
Doesn't know that love is blind.

She is like a skylark
Warbling some lovesick tune.
A tone deaf song-bird:
She's part cuckoo, she's part loon!

A self-deceiver, she will tell you
Love's a miracle.
Don't believe her. She's not logical.
She's lyrical!

Crazy lady, you'll learn in time:
That thrilling moment in the sun?
'Twas moonshine!

* A measure of vamping should abruptly interrupt the applause for the preceding
song and continue until the bewildered singer is about to protest. At that point,
the accompanist begins to sing.

Cabaret Songs
1. Who Could Have Known?

Words and Music by
DOMINICK ARGENTO

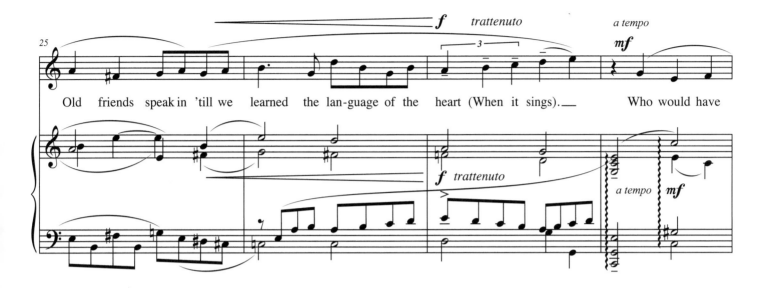

Old friends speak in 'till we learned the lan-guage of the heart (When it sings).___ Who would have

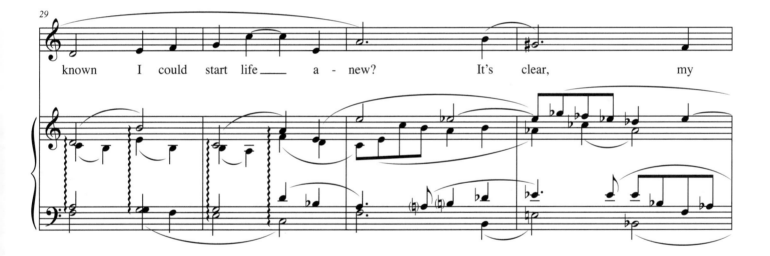

known I could start life___ a - new? It's clear, my

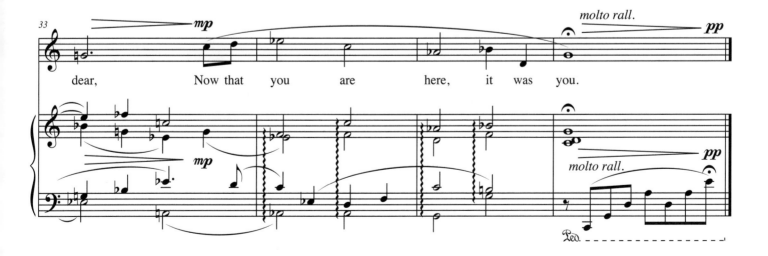

dear, Now that you are here, it was you.

2. You Are A Love Song

Simply and Tenderly (♩ = **66** *ca.*)   *poco rit.*

You are a love song__ I hear all__ the time. The words– short and

sim - ple:__ "I'm yours. You're mine." A song that will res - o - nate As

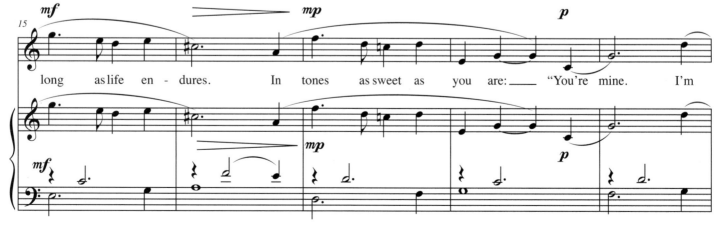

long as life en - dures. In tones as sweet as you are:__ "You're mine. I'm

3. The Luckiest Woman

I nev - er won the lot-ter-y,_____ Or a

prize of an - y worth. And yet to me I'll al - ways be The

luck - i - est wom-an on earth._____ I'm hope - less at Mo - nop - o - ly_____ And_ at

cards I vain-ly strive. But none-the-less, I must con-fess, I'm___ the

luck-i-est wom-an a-live._____ I wash the car;___ it's sure to rain.___ In-

vest my dough;__ right down the drain.___ Get a great job Mon-day; Tues-day: fired. Go to

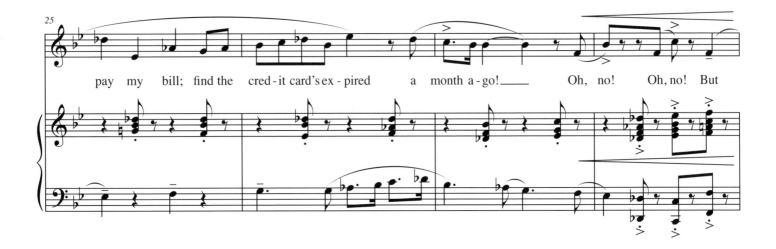

pay my bill; find the cred-it card's ex-pired a month a-go!___ Oh, no! Oh, no! But

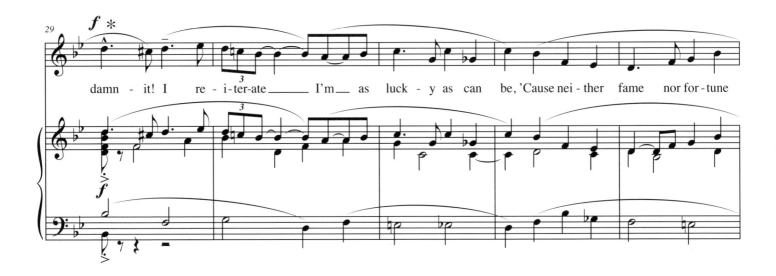

damn-it! I re-i-ter-ate___ I'm___ as luck-y as can be, 'Cause nei-ther fame nor for-tune

com-pen-sate___ For all that your love means___ to me._____

*As an ossia, the tempo may immediately be changed to quarter note equals 86 *circa*, in the manner of old vaudeville and music hall routines, expanding the accompaniment as desired, adding octaves to the left hand part, *etc.*.

4. Sai Tu Perchè

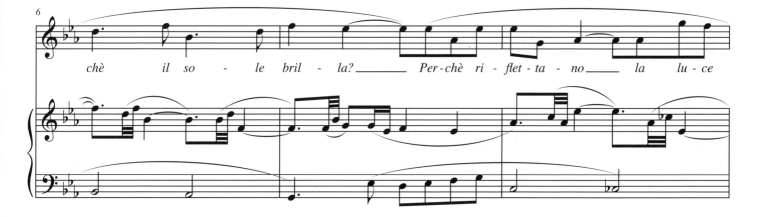

Sai tu per - chè la lu - na splen - de?_____ Sai tu per -

chè il so - le bril - la?_____ Per - chè ri - flet - ta - no_____ la lu - ce

d'un a - mor,___ La lu - ce d'un a - mo - re gran - de quan - t'e la mi - a.___ Non___

tro - vo mai pa - ro - le gius - te;___ Non___ po - trei dir - ti quan - to

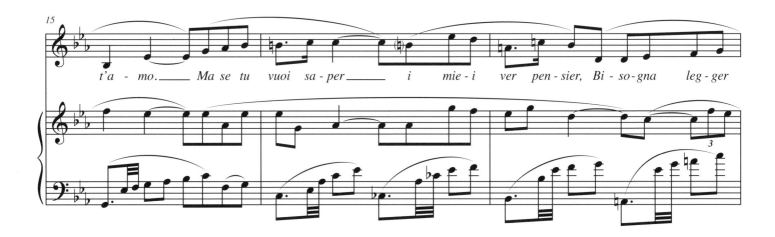

t'a - mo.___ Ma se tu vuoi sa - per___ i mie - i ver pen - sier, Bi - so - gna leg - ger

quel ch'è scrit - to___ nel cuo - re mi - o. Ed ec - co cos' è scrit - to___ "Sen - za

5a. You

I am at my hap-pi-est__ when-ev-er there's a chance to simp-ly gaze and gaze at

You!__ You're the rea-son__ that my heart's so light. The love__ that you show me__ makes my

fu-ture feel as bright As blue skies on a sun-ny day and school-boys on__ a hol-i-day. One

per - son makes me feel that way and that is you. Thanks to you I now be-lieve__ that

mir - a - cles come true: I ask you what you're think - ing.__ You re - ply: "It's al-ways you." At

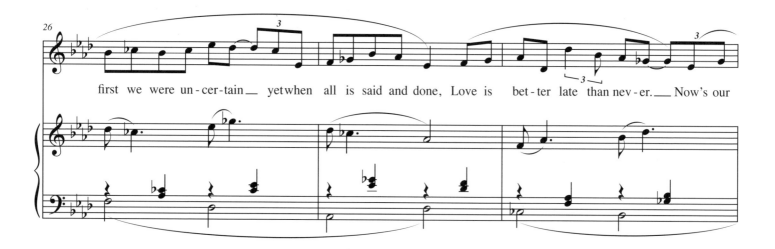

first we were un - cer - tain__ yet when all is said and done, Love is bet - ter late than nev - er.__ Now's our

mo - ment in the sun. O You,___ you are mu - sic,___ a tre - men - dous theme, Mere

words___ are un-worth-y___ to de - scribe so dear a dream, I'll nev - er have my fill of you, the

end-less joy___ and thrill of you, I'll keep right on un - til you too say "I'm in love with you!"

5b. Crazy Lady

* This measure of vamping should abruptly interrupt the applause for the preceding song and
continue until the bewildered singer is about to protest. At that point, the accompanist starts to sing.

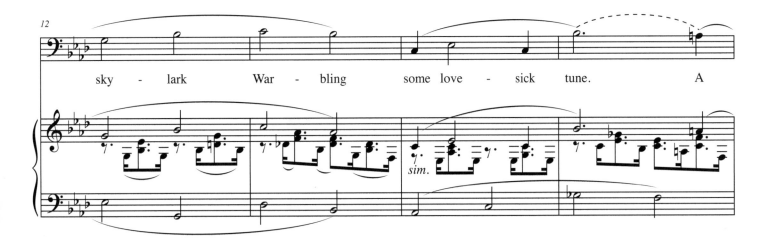

sky - lark War - bling some love - sick tune. A

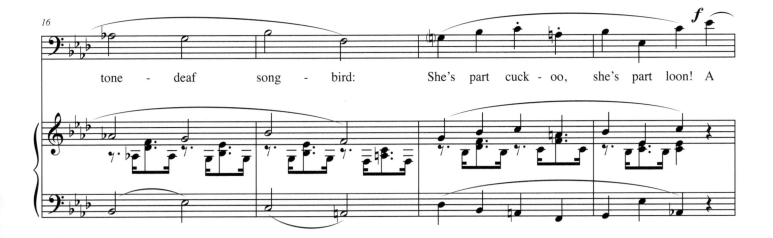

tone - deaf song - bird: She's part cuck - oo, she's part loon! A

self - de - ceiv - er, she will tell you Love's a mir - a-cle.

Don't be - lieve her. She's not log - i-cal.___ She's lyr - i - cal!

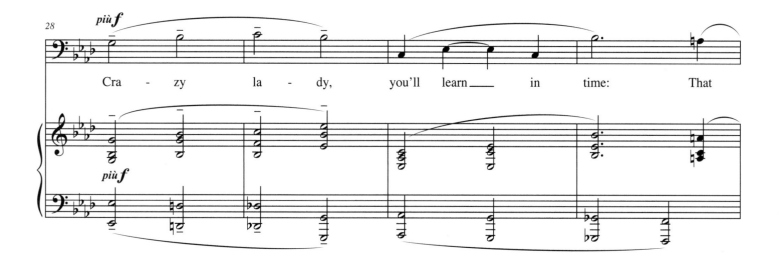

Cra - zy la - dy, you'll learn___ in time: That

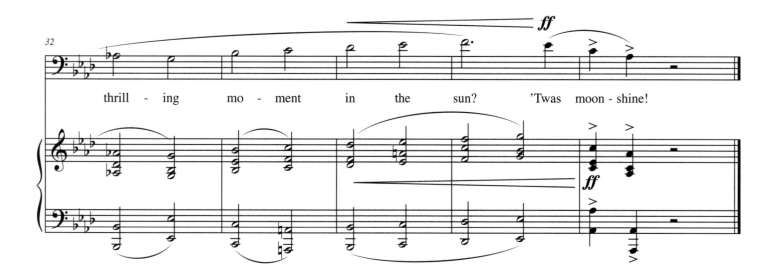

thrill - ing mo - ment in the sun? 'Twas moon - shine!

5c. You *and* Crazy Lady